BRITAIN IN OLD PH

THE LONDON BOROUGH OF
GREENWICH

COMPILED BY A GROUP FROM GREENWICH COMMUNITY
COLLEGE'S CREATIVE WRITING CLASS

GREENWICH COMMUNITY COLLEGE/
GREENWICH LOCAL HISTORY LIBRARY
SUTTON PUBLISHING LIMITED

Sutton Publishing Limited
Phoenix Mill · Thrupp · Stroud
Gloucestershire · GL5 2BU

First published 1997

Title page photograph: Hearse built at
Woolwich Arsenal, 1890s. See page 83.

British Library Cataloguing in Publication Data
A catalogue record for this book is available from the
British Library.

ISBN 0-7509-1377-0

Typeset in 10/12 Perpetua.
Typesetting and origination by
Sutton Publishing Limited.
Printed in Great Britain by
Ebenezer Baylis, Worcester.

General Wolfe statue, Greenwich Park.

CONTENTS

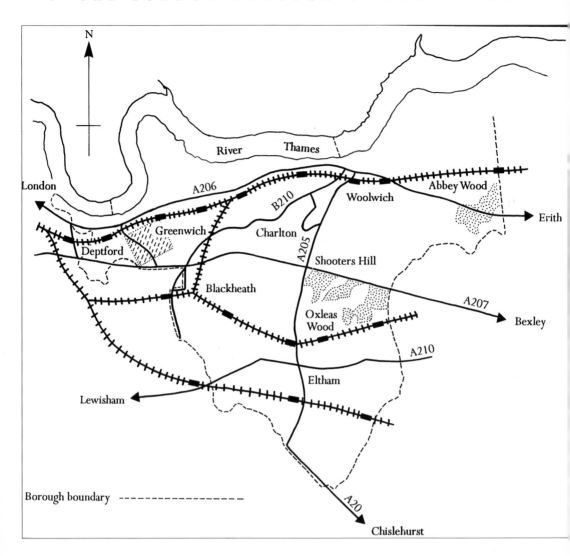

INTRODUCTION

When the Greenwich Community College invited our group of amateur writers to compile a book of old photographs of the London Borough of Greenwich, we were only too pleased to accept. Having lived in the borough all our lives, with memories of our own and a keen interest to find out more, we set about the task with enthusiasm. Limited by our ignorance and constrained by the availability of photographs, we feel nevertheless that this compilation does reflect the London Borough of Greenwich in all its richness and diversity. Every effort has been made to illustrate the colour and contrasts of Greenwich life over the last hundred years or so.

After much debate about its name, the London Borough of Greenwich was formed in 1965, an amalgamation of two Metropolitan boroughs. The first, Greenwich itself, included Charlton, Kidbrooke, and parts of Deptford and Blackheath. The second, Woolwich, brought in Plumstead, Abbey Wood and Eltham.

The London Borough of Greenwich is a very special place. It covers a vast area, from the wooded hills of Abbey Wood in the east, along the riverside conurbation of Plumstead, Woolwich, Charlton and Greenwich, to the wide open spaces of Blackheath and the palace and parks of Eltham. The whole area is now sprawling suburbia but it continues to have great attractions, not least because of its historical associations.

Greenwich itself, of course, has a name known throughout the world, because of Greenwich Mean Time and the Prime Meridian. Its links with astronomy and navigation are well established, and the royal influence is everywhere. Its proximity to central London, together with the historical attractions and its splendid natural features, have brought the tourists flocking to Greenwich in their thousands.

Eltham too can boast a royal palace and attractive parks and gardens. It is a residential suburb now, but the days when it was covered in farms are not far away, and evidence of those times is not difficult to find. The same is true of Kidbrooke, which was almost entirely rural until the 1930s, with market gardens, dairy farms and fields where rows of houses now stand.

Charlton, one of the smaller parishes of the borough, has managed to retain its village atmosphere. It has a well-preserved seventeenth-century church and is justifiably proud of its fine Jacobean mansion. Blackheath Village is more modern in origin, but it has a unique charm. Parts of Blackheath are in the Borough of Lewisham, since the boundary line passes through the village.

Today Woolwich is the headquarters of the London Borough of Greenwich, housing the Town Hall and other municipal buildings. In the past it was always the wealthiest of the parishes, mainly because of its military associations, and even today the town can be proud of its magnificent architectural heritage, as seen in such buildings as the Royal Arsenal, the Dockyards and the various military establishments.

Plumstead developed and grew because of the expansion of Woolwich in the nineteenth century. Despite its teeming population and the resultant large housing developments, Plumstead has, along with its neighbour Shooters Hill, managed to retain areas of peace and rural tranquillity in its woods, parks and commons. Abbey Wood is another neighbour of Plumstead which was for many years a quiet farming community. It is one of Greenwich's later developments, containing a mixture of private, co-operative and municipal housing.

By choosing photographs as our medium we can open only a small window on our past, but one that will hopefully demonstrate the variety of life in the London Borough of Greenwich. Many of the photographs were taken in living memory and all of them speak of the lives of ordinary folk – their work and leisure, their travel, and their homes and families. Some tell of a time long gone, when military and maritime interests were at the heart of these riverside communities, and industry brought affluence to some and a living wage to many more.

The production of this book would not have been possible without the superabundant help received from our Local History Library. Its staff provided most of the photographs we have used, together with a welter of assistance in verification and proofing. With the support we have also received from the Greenwich Community College, this has truly been a 'community' project and hopefully will repay in some small measure the debt we owe to the place we have made our home.

To be a Greenwich resident in the 1990s means being part of a diverse and exciting multi-cultural community, a green and leafy borough on the doorstep of London yet only a stone's throw from the Garden of England. We genuinely hope that both residents and visitors will enjoy this book and share with us the sense of pride we have in our borough, not just in its past but also in its future, and not least in its pivotal role in the forthcoming Millennium celebrations for the year 2000. Time marches on – may it ever be Greenwich Mean Time.

Hog Lane, later Nile Street, Woolwich, *c.* 1910. The street was later demolished to make way for the ferry approach road.

GREENWICH

The famous statue of General Wolfe overlooks the magnificent view of Greenwich from the Royal Park. This photograph was taken in the 1950s; nowadays, the lone car would not be allowed, and the Canary Wharf tower dominates the view.

Greenwich Royal Observatory. In 1675 Sir Christopher Wren was ordered 'to build, within our park at Greenwich, upon the highest ground, an observatory, with lodging rooms for our astronomical observator and assistant'. The building now houses an educational museum and a planetarium. The Royal Observatory has been moved to Cambridgeshire.

Flamsteed House, Greenwich Observatory, 1930s. The Wren Building was named after Charles II's first Astronomer Royal: John Flamsteed earned £100 per annum when he lodged here in 1675. The Time Ball on the roof, dropped at 1 p.m. every day, has been used by sailors on the Thames for more than 150 years, and is here the focus of attention for a group of schoolboys.

The 'Gate' Clock, erected 1851. This was one of the first electrically driven public clocks and is famous throughout the world for telling Greenwich Mean Time. The Meridian line passes nearby, where visitors can stand with one foot in each hemisphere! The decision to site the Prime Meridian at Greenwich was taken at the Washington Conference in 1884, when George Airey was Astronomer Royal.

Miss Anne Askew Davis, of East Lodge, poses in Greenwich Park in the 1880s. The Royal Observatory is just visible in the background. The park was first enclosed in 1433 by Humphrey, Duke of Gloucester. It was walled in the time of James I at a cost of £2,000.

The Boating Pool, Greenwich Park, 1940s. A popular place with children, there has always been a queue here in the summer months. Of particular interest are the vegetable allotments on the right. In the austere years during and after the Second World War, every spare piece of land was used for food production, and a Royal Park was no exception.

The training ship *Fame* outside the Queen's House, *c.* 1910. Thousands of boys from the Royal Hospital School must have trained over the years on this mock ship. It was eventually dismantled in 1933, when the school moved to Suffolk. The buildings then became the National Maritime Museum.

The deck of the training ship *Fame* as seen from the Queen's House. This view of the twin towers of the Royal Naval College, with the River Thames behind, is a well-known one. The site is of great historical interest. Henry VIII and his daughters Mary and Elizabeth were born at the Palace of Placentia, which originally stood here. Later, Sir Christopher Wren designed the building we see here as a Royal Hospital for Seamen. It was built between 1694 and 1752. The Royal Naval College took it over in 1873.

Boys of the Greenwich Royal Hospital School, *c.* 1910, in the buildings now used by the National Maritime Museum. Children had been educated here since 1807 in preparation for life in the Royal Navy. They were taught seamanship as well as the 'three Rs', but it was a harsh regime which included daily polishing of dormitory floors and scrubbing the dining rooms. Here dinner is about to be served for the 1000 boys then at the school.

The Hospital School Boys' Band, attracting the crowds at Greenwich in the 1920s or '30s. By 1933, when the school moved to Holbrook Estate in Suffolk, over 800 pupils attended, aged between eleven and fifteen years. Many of them went on to join the Navy.

The Ship Hotel, Greenwich, with the gates of Greenwich Pier behind, *c.* 1908. The poster advertises an auction of furniture and fittings to follow the demolition of part of the hotel and a snooker hall. The building was finally destroyed in the Blitz. Later, a dry dock was created on the site, and it is here that the famous tea-clipper *Cutty Sark* now stands, alongside Sir Francis Chichester's tiny yacht that sailed him round the world in 1967 – the *Gipsy Moth*.

West Gate, Royal Naval College, early 1900s. Before 1834, when this gate was moved to its present site, the whole area was full of narrow crowded streets, such as Fisher Alley (p. 21) which dated back to the Middle Ages. The two stone globes represent celestial and terrestrial spheres, with copper lines of longtitude and latitude still discernible.

A riverside scene at Greenwich in the 1950s. Highbridge and the huge jetty of Greenwich power station can be seen behind. A collier is moored alongside.

The Trafalgar Tavern, built in 1837. Once famous for its whitebait dinners, the riverside inn was frequented by such Victorian notables as Dickens, Thackeray and Cruikshank. Politicians dined here at the end of each parliamentary session. Threatened with demolition in the 1930s, the outbreak of the war won it a reprieve and it was eventually restored and re-opened in 1965.

Trinity Hospital, near Crane Street. Originally built as almshouses in 1616 by Henry Howard, Earl of Northampton, this white-fronted castellated building is overshadowed by the Greenwich power station and often overlooked by visitors, although it is only a few steps along the river walk. The inscription beneath the founder's coat-of-arms reads: 'Hospitale sancte et Individuae Trinitatis Grenwici 1616'; which means 'The Hospital of the Holy and Undivided Trinity'.

Fire by the river at East Greenwich, probably 1845, when Enderby's rope and canvas factory was destroyed by fire. The Enderby brothers, Charles, Henry and George, were well-known whalers and explorers. They founded the factory in 1823.

Ballast Quay, 1930. It was here that ships which had already discharged their cargo took on Blackheath gravel as ballast for their homeward journey. Ballast Quay has a fine Georgian terrace, a harbour-master's office, and the Cutty Sark Tavern which is on the site of the original Green Man.

St Alfege's Church, from a drawing of 1558. There has been a church on this site since before the twelfth century, marking the martyrdom of Alfege, Archbishop of Canterbury, who was taken prisoner by the raiding Danes. He refused to allow a ransom to be paid for his release and was beaten to death in 1012, supposedly on the spot where the church stands. The 'old church' in the picture collapsed in a great storm of 1710. It was one of the few to be rebuilt under the New Churches Act of 1712.

St Alfege's Church, c. 1900. The building, designed by Nicholas Hawksmoor in 1714, was 'placed in a Septum, or enclosure . . . to keep off Nastyness and Brutes'. John James encased the tower in 1730.

St Alfege's Church, demonstrating its dominant position in Greenwich town centre. This photo was taken in about 1900. Pepys and Evelyn, the seventeenth-century diarists, were regular attenders. Pepys wrote, 'by coach to Greenwich Church, where a good sermon, a fine church, and a great company of handsome women'. Greenwich Park station, on the left, was closed in 1917.

Greenwich Church Street, from a painting by W. Kerr. Boat menders on the cobbled street evoke long-gone days when the river was the chief means of transport. The spire of St Alfege's towers at the end of the street.

A Hanslip-Fletcher print of Greenwich Town, 1938. This is a view from the bottom of Crooms Hill, with the church and the White Hart Inn in the background. The Spreadeagle Tavern, reputedly the oldest in Greenwich, is among the buildings on the right. Now a restaurant and an antiques business, the Spreadeagle has retained its name and its reputation of service to visitors to Greenwich.

A public gathering by St Alfege's Church, 1852 (from a print in the *Illustrated London News*). The General Election took place on 10 July 1852 and was of interest in that Salomons, the first ever Jewish MP, was elected.

Crane Street, one of the oldest streets in Greenwich, *c.* 1900. It is a tiny, compact street, too narrow for traffic, between Park Row and Eastney Street. The people in the picture are posing outside the Yacht Tavern. Its age is unknown, though its present name dates from 1830. There has been an inn on this site for over 300 years, originally known as the Barley Mow, then renamed The Waterman's Arms from about 1805. Next door is the Curlew Yachting Club which was established in 1886 and is said to be the oldest club on the tideway.

The lane leading to Ship Street, from a print of 1830. Fisher Alley was one of a maze of medieval streets that made up the original Greenwich town centre. In the 1830s the streets were all swept away to create Greenwich Market, King William Walk, College Approach, etc., a development designed by Joseph Kay on behalf of Greenwich Hospital Estates.

Church Street in the 1890s, with its distinctive weather-boarded buildings. This is a good example of early housing in Greenwich. A waterman with his pipe stands in the foreground.

Billingsgate Street. Nobody knows the origin of the street name (though many have hazarded guesses). The street was demolished in 1938 and replaced by a large housing estate beside the river.

The Coach and Horses Inn, the market pub in Turnpin Lane. This, the most ancient alley in Greenwich, was once twice its present length. It derived its name from the 'turn-pin', a barrier which controlled access in the seventeenth century – an early traffic-calming measure!

Tuskar Street, 1937. The houses were decorated to celebrate the coronation of King George VI.

Straightsmouth, 1930s. Liz Lloyd is standing at the door of her home, 80 Straightsmouth, where she still lives.

Straightsmouth, 1930s. A motor car was an unusual sight, and attracted admirers. Liz Lloyd is sitting in the driver's seat. The row of cottages has changed not at all up to the present day.

Trams in Church Street, *c.* 1935. A reliable, if rattly, form of transport which served the community until 1952. The distinctive architectural features of Burtons (men's outfitters) can be seen in the background.

A tram picks up passengers outside St Alfege's on its way to Abbey Wood, *c*. 1935. The dangers to passengers of having to board and alight in the middle of the road were increasing: this was the main reason why trams had to go.

Dreadnought Seamen's Hospital, mid-1930s. The *Dreadnought*, originally a hospital ship, came ashore to Greenwich in 1870. Bicycles, pedestrians, and a tram highlight the main modes of transport sixty years ago.

Romney Road. By the 1950s, traffic was becoming heavier and Greenwich was, and still is, used as a through-road to London. The architectural skills of Joseph Kay were responsible for these buildings of the 1830s.

The Greenwich Union Workhouse, c. 1900. Built in 1840 to house up to 1200 destitute or infirm men, women and children, the workhouse was the last resort of the desperate. Families were separated, on the grounds that the poor were 'apt to disregard . . . conventional proprieties'. St Alfege's Hospital later shared the site, which is now occupied by Greenwich District Hospital.

The Clarence Steam Printing Works, before the First World War. The next-door building, housing Addis & Usherwood, general stores, has had to be shored up, giving the scene a rather desolate air. Clarence Street is now known as College Approach.

St Mary's Church, Greenwich, about to be demolished in 1933. The statue of King William now stands on this site, at the lower end of Greenwich Park.

Demolition of St Mary's in progress, 1933. It is interesting to note the rather primitive method of rubbish disposal, i.e. wicker baskets. The Maritime Museum (then used as the Royal Hospital School) can be seen in the background.

The Powder Magazine, from a 1794 print. This gunpowder store stood on the western shore of Blackwall Point and was cause for complaint as early as 1759, when a petition from local inhabitants demanded its removal because of the potential danger. Gunpowder was later stored in hulks moored in the river, for greater safety.

West Greenwich fire station, 1884. The fire station was sited near Royal Hill, in Grove Street. The engines were of course horse-drawn, and carried a steam pump.

Firemen at the opening ceremony of the East Greenwich fire station (pictured below), 1902. By October of that year, every Greenwich fire station was equipped with one steam fire engine, one horsed escape, one manual escape, one hose cart and four horses. There were twenty-two street fire alarms within the borough, and seven more on order.

East Greenwich fire station, which closed in 1985. This building has since been turned into a hotel. It is near the Blackwall Tunnel approach road. The new fire station is a little further east along the Woolwich Road.

Park Vista, Greenwich. The neat, elegant frontage of one house denotes the gentility of the area between the wars. It is possible that this gate and railings were stripped away during the Second World War to provide scrap iron for war work – only to lie unused behind the Woolwich Arsenal walls!

Plume of Feathers pub, Park Vista. This is one of the oldest pubs in Greenwich, with records going back to the first quarter of the eighteenth century. It probably stood on the old main road to Woolwich which ran beneath the Queen's House. The Meridian line slices neatly through the pub.

The approach to Blackwall Tunnel was opened in May 1897 by the Prince and Princess of Wales. Its construction was a remarkable feat of engineering, led by Sir A.R. Binney, especially so because very few people were killed in the five years it took to build. Over 335,000 horse-drawn vehicles used the tunnel in its first year, plus innumerable pedestrians. For many seeking work in the dockyards it solved the problem of how to cross the Thames. Buses have always used the tunnel, but trams never went through. The original tunnel is now used for north-bound traffic only – and certainly no pedestrians! A south-bound tunnel, built alongside, was opened in 1967. Such is the volume of traffic that there has even been a proposal, in 1990, to build a third tunnel.

Feathers Place, in the days when this building housed the boys of the Roan School. It is now used by the National Maritime Museum. The first Roan school was built in 1677 with money left by John Roan to benefit the children of Greenwich. Both boys and girls had schools built for them in 1877 but as they were fee-paying they hardly lived up to the founder's intention. In 1944 the schools became voluntary-aided grammar schools and children were selected according to academic ability. Since 1977 the school has been a mixed comprehensive, using the sites on Maze Hill and Westcombe Park Road.

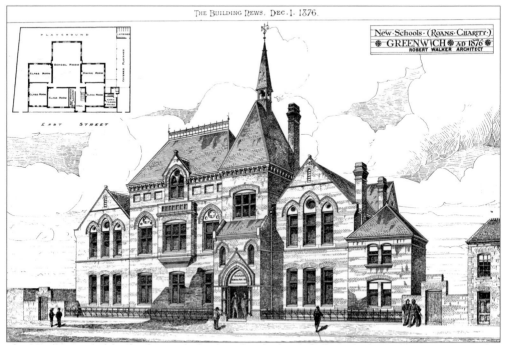

The 'new' Roan Girls' School, 1877. The three hundred girls had to pay fees, so it was very much a middle-class establishment. Earlier, in 1814, it had been suggested that girls should benefit from the John Roan charity, so a school was set up – and the girls were entrusted with making stockings and shirts for the boys!

Roan School for Girls, Devonshire Drive, before it joined with the boys' school and became a comprehensive school in 1977. The girls used this building for a hundred years. They had little contact with the Roan Boys, except at the annual Founder's Day service in St Alfege's Church. This school building has recently been redesigned as luxury apartments.

Egerton Drive, off Devonshire Drive, in the early 1960s. This smart road with its imposing villas was built in about 1830.

George Frederick Franklin standing behind his sister and brother outside their Greenwich home in Thames Street in the early 1900s.

A Greenwich football team of the 1920s. Seated, second from left, is Frank Nicholson who later worked in Woolwich power station.

A Greenwich wedding, Christmas Day 1925. Frank Nicholson's football days may well have been over when he married Nora Franklin at St George's Church, Kirkside Road. The photograph was taken outside the bride's home in Combedale Road. The bridesmaid on the left is Nora's sister, Iris.

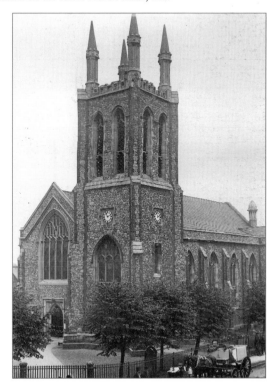

Christ Church, Greenwich, *c.* 1900. This Victorian Gothic church was built in 1848. It is still there on the main Woolwich Road and well known in the borough as the Christ Church Forum.

Greenwich streets celebrate the coronation of Queen Elizabeth II, June 1953. Above is a group of friends and neighbours from Glaisher Street. Below is Straightsmouth; these houses still remain.

Straightsmouth victory celebrations after the First World War (above) and the Second World War (below). Many families lived for generations in this same Greenwich street, which is overlooked by the ancient church of St Alfege. In the photograph above can be seen, on the left, Miss O'Connor, Mary Dixon, Miss Lower and Elizabeth Slack (later Mrs Hammond). Albert Leay is the first boy seated on the left. The Smith children are grouped, centre, and Mr and Mrs Slack are standing far right, in front of Mrs Coutts.

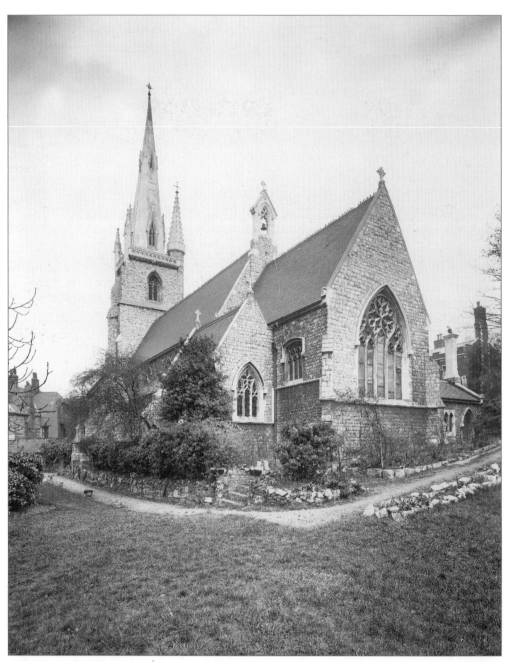

Church of Our Lady Star of the Sea, Crooms Hill. This was the first Roman Catholic church in Greenwich, built in 1851 by W.W. Wardell. Much of the interior decoration is reputed to be by Pugin. A delightful story tells of a Catholic lady, Mrs North, who vowed she would build a church to honour Our Lady Star of the Sea if her two sons could be saved from drowning. The pleasure boat they were on had capsized near Greenwich and thrown the family into the river. The boys were rescued and later grew up to be priests. Canon Richard North completed the building of the church after many setbacks. A great deal of money for the construction was raised by the Catholics among the Naval pensioners at Greenwich Hospital who had previously had to worship in a tiny chapel behind Park Vista.

Gloucester Circus, 1950s. One of the most elegant roads in Greenwich, this Georgian crescent faces a tranquil green square. Its beauty is now somewhat diminished by the ever-present parked motor cars.

Crooms Hill, one of Greenwich's oldest roads. It winds up from St Alfege's Church to Blackheath and contains many interesting buildings which have, over the years, attracted a number of substantial citizens, including Benjamin Waugh (1839–1908), the founder of the NSPCC, and Poet Laureate Cecil Day Lewis who lived for many years at no. 6 until his death in 1972.

Sisters from the Ursuline Convent, Crooms Hill, standing outside the Presbytery of Our Lady Star of the Sea.

The Gazebo, Crooms Hill, built in the grounds of no. 52, The Grange. The original house dates back to Tudor or even medieval times. This red-brick gazebo, which overlooks Greenwich Park, was designed in 1672 by Robert Hooke, and significantly restored in 1972.

BLACKHEATH & KIDBROOKE

The entrance to Greenwich Park from Folly Pond, Blackheath. This is the starting point for the annual London Marathon. The large trees pictured here were lost in the celebrated 'hurricane' of October 1987.

Ranger's House, Blackheath, from a Victorian print. The core of the house was originally built in the early 1700s for Admiral Sir Francis Hosier. It was later inherited by the 4th Earl of Chesterfield who extended it and created a garden of exotic fruit. From 1807 it was the Ranger's House for the Ranger of Greenwich Park, before opening as a museum in 1974. It is now part of the Iveagh Bequest and houses the Suffolk Collection, with many paintings by William Larkin.

A view from above the Ranger's House, looking over Greenwich Park towards London. The Meridian line passes through the house.

Prince of Wales Pond, Blackheath, 1950s.
Model boat enthusiasts have used this pond for
years. A line of wartime prefabs is just visible in
the background.

Blackheath entrance to Greenwich Park, *c.* 1900. Donkey rides continue to provide a weekend treat for
children, even in the 1990s. Here, it appears that adults too are joining in the fun. All the ladies are riding
side-saddle.

The Prince of Wales pond, looking towards All Saints' Church, Blackheath. Such a photograph, empty of traffic and people, could rarely be taken now, except perhaps in the early hours of a winter morning.

All Saints', Blackheath. The church is a well-known and attractive landmark for travellers to and from London. The spire of St John's can be seen on the horizon. Blackheath Village dips to the photographer's right, and the border between the boroughs of Greenwich and Lewisham is behind him.

Blackheath in the early years of this century. The open spaces of Blackheath have long attracted visitors. Here, women and children watch and play while the West Kent Wanderers enjoy a game of cricket. Fairs have been held on the heath since the seventeenth century.

Skating on the Prince of Wales pond, early 1900s. Because of its proximity to the city, Blackheath was the meeting place of kings and crowds for many centuries. It was also a favourite review ground for military displays. Historical figures such as Wat Tyler, Henry VIII and Charles II have links with Blackheath.

The Paragon, Blackheath. This elegant row of fourteen houses with their linking colonnades was designed in the late 1700s by Michael Searles, the architect responsible for Gloucester Circus in Greenwich.

Damage to the Paragon during the Second World War. Now skilfully restored, the Paragon houses still proudly stand in their prime position facing across Blackheath.

The entrance to Morden College, in a secluded corner of Blackheath. The college is a fine building, possibly designed by Wren in 1695, and founded by Sir John Morden, a merchant, as a safe haven for 'poor, sober and discreet merchants' who had lost all at sea. Morden's charity still offers accommodation to the elderly.

Woodlands, Mycenae Road, 1934. The house was then a convent for the Little Sisters of the Assumption. The London Borough of Greenwich bought this building and the one behind (the Novitiate House, now Mycenae House) in 1967. Woodlands is now the Local History Library and an Art Gallery. Mycenae House is a community centre.

The Royal Standard public house, Blackheath, *c.* 1915. Known to locals as The Standard, this area of shops and businesses at the junction of the Old Dover Road, Stratheden Road and Westcombe Hill is nowadays always busy with traffic. Barclays Bank still occupies the building on the right. The open-topped buses would be en route to central London.

St John's Church, Blackheath, whose spire can also be seen in the top picture. The church today still looks very much as it did at the turn of the century.

The fields of rural Kidbrooke, used as farmland for centuries, before development in the 1930s. The Black Death of 1347 is supposed to have wiped out the little community, and the ancient parish church of St Nicholas, on the corner of Brook Lane, fell into disuse because 'no parishioner dwells there'.

Kidbrooke in the 1930s when the farms and fields of this rural community were being taken over by housing estates, changing its character for ever.

Apple-picking in Chandler's Orchard, Kidbrooke, just before the First World War. The orchard continued to produce fruit and vegetables for local people right up to the Second World War.

Chandler's Farm House, Kidbrooke Lane, 1914. Farmland and orchards once covered this whole area, but estates and roads, built around the Rochester Way, have changed it beyond recognition.

CHARLTON

A view from Maryon Park towards the Thames at Charlton, c. 1900. Siemen's factory, where submarine cables were manufactured, is clearly visible, as is a three-masted ship on the left. The Thames Barrier now crosses the river at this point. The school on the right, now an annexe of Woolwich College, was originally Maryon Park School.

Lunch break at Siemen Brothers telegraph works, *c.* 1910. Wives and children would often meet the men at the gate to give them their lunch. Siemen's provided work for thousands of people for fifty years.

Official opening of the Guild Estate, Charlton, July 1921. This was Greenwich borough council's first estate in Charlton and 164 houses were built on the Fairfield.

St Luke's Church, Charlton, early this century. The church was rebuilt in 1630 with money left for that purpose by Sir Adam Newton, builder of Charlton House.

Charlton Village, looking east towards Woolwich, *c.* 1900. St Luke's Church is just behind and to the left of the photographer. The Bugle Horn public house is on the right.

Charlton House, from an early print. A splendid example of Jacobean architecture, the house was built in 1607. It is now used as a community centre.

A modern photograph of Charlton House, showing the stone gateway which was once the entry-gate to the house. The house was the location for Alan Bennett's *A Question of Attribution*, shown on BBC TV in October 1991.

Shirley House, Charlton, which opened as a preparatory school for boys in 1904. Henry Storr, who later became a curate at St Luke's, was the first headmaster. Colonel Robertson took over as head in the early 1920s, and the school became known as Cherry Orchard School until its closure in 1936. Greenwich Borough Council then bought the estate for housing. It has retained its name of Cherry Orchard.

The Heights, Charlton, c. 1895, was once the site of William Sheppard's market garden off Lansdowne Lane, which had two large ponds big enough to row on.

Charlton's greyhound stadium was in existence from 1938 to 1971. A man with a bell started the races and tickets cost 3s 9d, 2s 8d or 1s 6d.

An early day-trip from the Bugle Horn public house, Charlton, in a horse-drawn charabanc.

The last trams line up in Penhall Road, 1952. 'Last Tram Week', 29 June–5 July, was announced on large posters on the upper decks of the trams, and you could buy souvenir tickets for 2*s* 6*d*.

Charlton station, after suffering severe bomb damage during the Second World War.

The Anchor and Hope public house, now run by a brewery chain. It derives its name from the days when sailing barges and brigs came to Charlton to load ballast: their skippers may well have had to 'anchor' and then 'hope' for a change in the weather. For many years it was a well-known riverside centre, and starting point for the watermen's races.

Cory barges at Charlton, c. 1980. William Cory & Sons Ltd was a river firm that initially carried coal and later developed into a thriving barge-building business in the late nineteenth century.

WOOLWICH

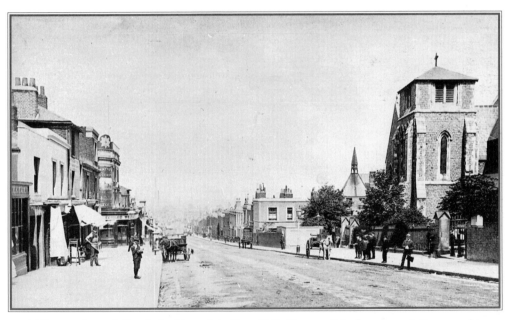

Wellington Street, before the building of the Town Hall. The site of the future town hall — opened in 1906 — is further down the hill, on the left. St John's Church (demolished 1938) is on the right.

Wellington Street, with new Town Hall, *c*. 1906. The freehold was bought for £15,880 and was the first use of a Compulsory Powers Order to purchase land for municipal purposes. The site was originally intended for use as a new market place, but following opposition, the public baths, a library, the police station and the fine Town Hall, designed by Mr A. Brumwell-Thomas, were all built on this piece of land.

Rectory Place, before the Second World War. Many of the original houses were occupied by the families of army officers and by prosperous tradesmen. John Wilson, the widely respected minister of the Woolwich Baptist Tabernacle, lived here. He and Charles Grinling together organized the Woolwich Council of Social Service and, in 1925, the Invalid Children's Association. A nearby road is now named after him.

The Grand Opening of Market Street Baths, 1894. The building is now used by the University of Greenwich for the Students' Union.

The Hippodrome, Wellington Street. The theatre became a cinema (very popular with the soldiers from the garrison) in the 1920s. Then, it cost four old pence for a wooden gallery seat and peanut shells were said to be ankle-deep.

This playbill from the Hippodrome's music hall dates back to 1909.

Beresford Square, Woolwich, before the First World War. Originally open common land surrounded by low-roofed cottages, it received official market status in 1888 and has continued as a thriving open market ever since. Until 1939 it was often the scene of popular meetings and demonstrations.

Beresford Square market, early 1930s. This part was known as the High Pavement. The Arsenal main gate can be seen in the background. Gas lamps, and later naptha flares, were used after dark until electric lights were introduced. Saturday night was the busiest time when food was sold off cheaply. On Sundays local preachers and political speakers could be heard in the square. The market square is now traffic-free.

The last tram in Woolwich, 1 July 1952. The no. 46 ran from Woolwich to Eltham, via Woolwich Common. Trolley-buses continued for another seven years until they too were discontinued and replaced by diesel-powered buses.

Main gate, Woolwich Arsenal, probably before the First World War. A horse-drawn tram with open roof is clearly visible. The lack of market stalls indicates that this is a Sunday scene.

Beresford Square, early 1950s. The Arsenal main gate is on the right, with Holy Trinity Church next to it. The Century cinema was one of many in the Woolwich area. Jolting trolley-buses make their way down Beresford Street. They lasted until 1959. A pet stall on the right sold birds, kittens and puppies and all the paraphernalia required by pet owners.

Holy Trinity Church, Beresford Square. This elegant eighteenth-century octagonal church was demolished in 1958 to make way for road widening between Plumstead and the Woolwich Ferry.

A modern view of Beresford Square market, *c.* 1960. All sorts of goods are sold, from rugs and curtains to luggage and toys, as well as traditional foodstuffs such as fruit, vegetables and fish. A local legend tells of the infamous Maud Skinner, prostitute, who bathed naked in the horse trough outside the Ordnance Arms after one of her many forcible ejections from said public house!

Ropeyard Rails, before demolition in 1935. This was the 'rope-walk' that ran parallel to Beresford Street and alongside the river where, during manufacture, hundreds of yards of rope were laid out in straight lines. The area has a chequered history, and for a time its name was synonymous with squalor and crime – the 'Dust Hole'. In its place there is now a river walkway and a small industrial estate.

Green's End, 1950s. Once known as Sappers' Green, this corner of Woolwich has seen considerable changes in recent years. The Town Hall can be seen in the distance, and Beresford Square market is behind the photographer. The area is now a pedestrian precinct, so the zebra crossings are no more.

Green's End, early 1930s, looking towards Beresford Square. The shop on the left is the Home and Colonial (provisions) Stores; next door is Purvess, grocer, famed for its coffee and tea. The large shop opposite specialized in mourning clothes.

'The Smoke Hole', by Woolwich Arsenal station, 1920s. Mr Thomas Brown, a local tailor (in top hat), campaigned for years to have the railway covered at this point where the trains entered the station (seen in the background). Ever since the railway line had been built in 1849, the space between New Road and Green's End had been 'a yawning gulf surrounded by a brick wall', into which the trains would belch their dense black smoke.

The closure of the Smoke Hole, February 1912 (Mr Brown in top hat again). Campaigners were finally successful in getting the hole covered after the electrification of the railway in 1926. The LCC bestowed the name General Gordon Place on the area, and Mr Brown's dream of having an attractive square with promenade and flowers has at last been realized, in the 1990s.

The original Woolwich Arsenal station, built 1849. The offices and entrance were in what is now Vincent Road. Both the Arsenal and the Dockyard stations were built on former sandpits. Regular services to central London and Kentish seaside resorts were provided to local people for the first time.

The second Woolwich Arsenal station, built 1900. This one faced Woolwich New Road and became a focal point for travellers of all kinds, including soldiers, day-trippers and the crowds of hop-pickers who journeyed into Kent for their annual working holiday. The attractive hansom cabs survived until the mid-thirties.

Cattle pens at Woolwich Arsenal station, before 1930. Cattle brought by rail were herded into these pens before being driven through the streets for slaughter in butchers' yards. The practice was discontinued in the 1930s when a central abattoir was built. This is now the site of a commuters' car park.

Woolwich Dockyard station, 1958, with Fred Lowe, booking clerk. Cheap trips are advertised to Sheerness, Herne Bay and Folkestone.

Powis Street, early this century. Both these photographs tell of a Woolwich long gone, in an era of prosperity and stability. Several of the stores, for example Cuffs, Garretts, RACS, Pryce (printers), David Greig's, Hedley Vicars (butchers), Joe Lyons, Birts (jewellers), were in business for decades and catered for shoppers from miles around. Powis Street is now almost entirely pedestrianized and its shops struggle in an increasingly competitive environment.

Hedley Vicars, butchers, Powis Street, here celebrating their centenary in 1951. In pre-refrigeration days, meat was sold off cheaply on Saturday evenings. Hot saveloys, faggots and pease pudding were sold from the small cart. The shop finally closed when the area was redeveloped in the 1960s.

Hare Street, 1920s. This is the view looking north towards the ferry, and it is very much changed today. Then, it was a bustling shopping street with businesses such as Lipton's (provisions), G. Robinson (drapers), Alvarez (milliners), Pegram's (tea-merchants), Arthur's (tailors), Barron's (bootmakers), and Sackett's (ironmongers).

Hare Street, at the opening of the Woolwich Free Ferry, March 1889. The London County Council provided the Free Ferry to link the north and south banks of the Thames at Woolwich. It is still running and still free. This is the north end of Hare Street, nearest to the river. The VIPs in the foreground wear top hats for the occasion. The pub on the right is Plaisteds (now the Coopers Arms), reputedly the oldest pub in Woolwich, dating back to 1790.

Inaugural crossing of the Woolwich Free Ferry, 1889. This boat, the *Gordon*, was named after General Gordon of Khartoum, who was born in Woolwich. The *Gordon* could carry 1000 passengers and cost £15,000 to build. Together with her sister ship, the *Duncan*, she served until 1923.

A 'Penny Ferry' at Woolwich, probably at the turn of the century. Paddle steamers like these were largely ousted after the inauguration of the free ferry in 1889, but continued to operate until 1908. The familiar red-sailed Thames barges can be seen on the tideway.

The *William Squires* ferry boat, after 1923. This side-loading paddle ferry took over from the *Gordon* and the *Duncan* and was in use until after the Second World War. It was named after William John Squires, a local printer who was twice mayor of Woolwich and chair of the Woolwich Equitable Building Society.

Bellwater Gate, near the ferry approach. Originally a coal wharf, this slipway was used as a starting point for a passenger river-boat service. It took two to three hours to reach the city from here, depending on the tide. The cobbles came from ballast left by ships at the wharves. This is now the site of the Waterfront Leisure Centre.

Market Hill, 1920s. This became the old ferry approach, where traffic waited to board the ferry (to the left).

Woolwich High Street, near the ferry. Some of these buildings were built in the eighteenth century, when the High Street was the main road from Greenwich. Although extensively restored these buildings are still in rather poor condition.

View of Woolwich Dockyard, before the First World War, from the north bank of the Thames. An ocean-going vessel, a paddle-steamer ferry and the dockyard clock-tower are clearly visible.

Meeting House Lane and Woolwich High Street, 1880. In 1912 these houses were demolished to make way for the power station, and no trace of them remains.

The aftermath of the *Princess Alice* disaster, 1878. This picture shows the search for bodies in the filthy water of the Thames. A collier hit the pleasure boat as it returned from a day trip and 700 people died. There is a memorial in St Mary's Church.

St Mary's, parish church of Woolwich. Built in 1732 near the site of the original twelfth-century church, St Mary's was enlarged and restored in the late nineteenth century. It contains a fine organ and several interesting monuments, principally to artillery officers. Tombs include that of Andrew Schalch, director of the gun foundry, and Tom Cribb the celebrated boxer who died in 1848.

St Mary's when the church was used solely for worship, *c.* 1900. Part of it is now used by Greenwich Social Services, the side aisles having been partitioned for the purpose. In the early sixties the Revd Nicholas Stacey worked hard to raise funds for restoration and to attract more worshippers.

Bowater Road, Woolwich Dockyard area, 1950s. Siemen's buildings and various dockyard units can be seen behind. The houses with lighter roofs were probably repaired after bomb damage. Now demolished, the whole area is an industrial estate today.

Castile Road backyard, demolished in 1972. These tiny houses had no bathrooms, hence the zinc bath hanging on the outside wall.

Kingsman Street scullery, before demolition in 1972. This would double as kitchen and bathroom for the family.

Main Guard House, Dial Square, Woolwich Arsenal, built in 1788. This is one of the elegant neo-classical buildings inside the Arsenal walls. The famous Arsenal football team's original name was Dial Square.

Mrs Lloyd George on a morale-boosting visit to Woolwich Arsenal during the First World War. Thousands of women were employed in the Arsenal during the war, many working with explosives in the Danger Buildings, which turned their skin yellow and earned the women the nickname 'canaries'.

The Woolwich Infant, photographed in the Arsenal. This 35-ton muzzle-loading naval gun was built at Woolwich in 1870. During its practice run to the Mediterranean on board HMS *Thunderer* it exploded, killing many men. As a result, the barrels were strengthened and it became a breech-loader for use on land. The Russian Tsar saw fifty such guns being assembled when he visited the Royal Arsenal. A pub on the Plumstead Road takes its name from the gun.

A hearse built at the Woolwich Arsenal, 1890s. Made of cast iron, it was used at the funerals of important employees. Holy Trinity Church, Beresford Square is in the background.

Woolwich Common, early 1900s. A hansom cab waits outside one of the many imposing houses that faced the common. Several were occupied by army officers. They have now been replaced by a large housing estate.

Women workers at Woolwich during the First World War. A crêche for the Arsenal encouraged women to work there, many in the Danger Buildings, filling shells. The dockyard buildings were used to manufacture military equipment, such as the saddles pictured below.

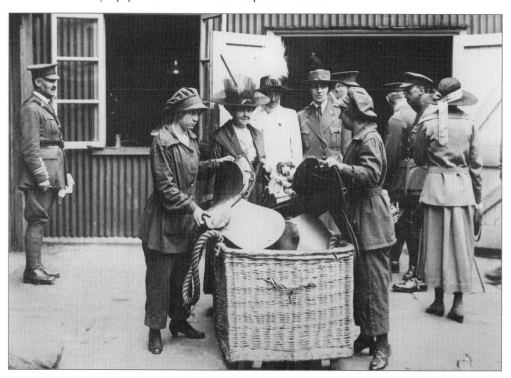

The Royal Artillery 'At Home', 1960. A popular local event, this was used as a public relations exercise for the RA. The long façade of Artillery barracks is in the background.

The African War Memorial, Frances Street. Erected by the Royal Army Service Corps in memory of those who died in the Boer War (1899–1902), the memorial was sadly neglected and moved to the Service Corps headquarters.

Royal Electrical and Mechanical Engineers' barracks, Woolwich, following a bombing raid during the Blitz. The engineers were stationed at Green Hill, near Repository Road.

Day of Prayer, Woolwich, 1942, for the men of the Royal Electrical and Mechanical Engineers.

Sandy Hill in the snow, probably before the First World War. It is one of the many steep streets of Woolwich on the geological formation known as the Thames Terraces. Sandy Hill, named after the sand pits of the last century, has changed little since this photograph was taken.

Woolwich New Road, at about the same date. Sandy Hill is the road off to the left. The New Road is an important route from Beresford Square to Woolwich Common. The spire of St Peter's Roman Catholic Church (built at the turn of the century for the many Irish immigrants) can be seen in the background.

A dancing bear, Woolwich Common, probably
c. 1890. This bear was often seen at local fairs.
When not performing he was kept in the cellar
of a nearby pub. The common continues to host
a number of fairs every year – but no bears.

Children from Class 1, Elizabeth Street School, North Woolwich. Since 1965 North Woolwich has been
part of the Borough of Newham, but at the time of the photograph this London County Council school
was most definitely under the auspices of Woolwich Borough. Marion Shaw, who wrote about the school,
is seated in the second row, fifth from the right.

ABBEY WOOD

Bostall Woods from Wickham Lane. The woods, purchased by the London County Council in the 1890s, are still there, but the surrounding area is now busy roads and housing estates, a very different picture from this rural 'Day of the Fair' scene. Robert Bloomfield, poet of Woolwich, describes Bostall Woods as 'brown heaths that upward rise and overlook the winding Thames'.

Bostall Hill from Wickham Lane, *c.* 1910. Stanley's grocers stands on the corner at no. 1 Blenheim Terrace.

Abbey Wood tram terminus, *c.* 1920. A return fare from Abbey Wood to Victoria was 8*d*, and the trams ran at two to four minute intervals.

King's Norton factory, First World War. Women workers were encouraged to join in the fun of the annual Sports Day. During the war this was one of the many factories requisitioned by the government for specific war work, in this case filling shells with lyddite.

Royal visit to King's Norton, during the First World War. Here, King George V, Queen Mary and Princess Mary help to boost the morale of the munitions workers.

Rural scenes in Abbey Wood from a century ago. The area derives its name from the Abbey of Lesnes, founded by Richard de Lucy in the twelfth century, and well excavated in the early 1900s. Ancient ruins still survive. Abbey Wood was a sparsely populated farming community until the Bostall Estate was built between 1900 and 1914. The cottages, above, nestle sleepily in Bostall Woods, and the picture below shows Scots pines being felled on Bostal Heath in 1908. The timber was used for telegraph poles and railway sleepers.

PLUMSTEAD

&

SHOOTERS HILL

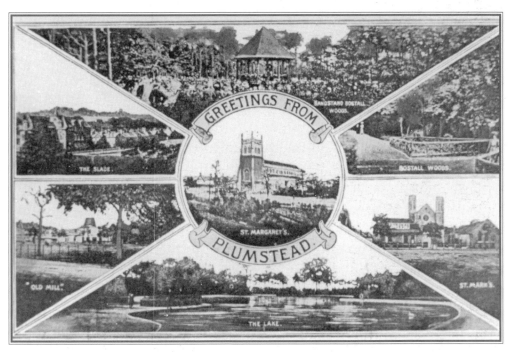

An unlikely greetings card from Plumstead, probably dating back to the 1920s. Bostall Woods and the lake on Plumstead Common are featured, as is the Old Mill, and the churches of St Margaret and St Mark.

Protesters on Plumstead Common, 1860. When the owners (Queen's College, Oxford) attempted to enclose parts of the common and gave the army permission to use it as a training ground, there was uproar. John de Morgan was imprisoned for leading the protest. Eventually an act of parliament in 1877 saved the common and it was later purchased by the Borough of Woolwich.

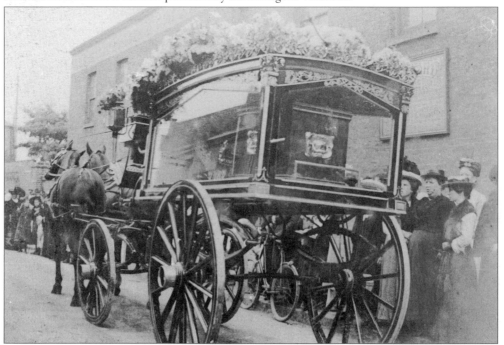

A Victorian funeral in Plumstead. The ornate hearse belonged to Oscar Berry, funeral directors of Herbert Road.

A Woolwich borough council horse and cart at the Slade, Plumstead Common. The public lavatories behind the railings were built, at public request, in the mid-1930s. Greenslade school, formerly the Slade School, a London School Board building of 1884, is in the background.

The Ship Inn, Plumstead Common Road, early this century. It was completely rebuilt in 1931 but still retains a late nineteenth-century appearance.

King's Warren School, Plumstead Common, *c*. 1920. The school was opened in September 1913 and became affectionately known as the Brown School because of its uniform. For fee-paying girls the cost was £3 6*s* 8*d* per term. In the early years only a minority stayed on until the sixth form. Since 1967 the school has been an all girls' comprehensive, renamed Plumstead Manor.

The Art Room, King's Warren, 1920. Seated at the front, left to right are Connie Moore, Gladys Bussey, Vera Lindsay and Doris Penny. In the second row (right) are Jenny Field and Kathleen Bulpitt.

Staff at King's Warren School, *c*. 1913. Seated centre, is the head, Miss Bartram, who taught religion. On her right is Miss Balding, the Latin teacher, and immediately behind them are Miss Gumley (French) and Miss Martin (art). Standing on the far right is the maths teacher, Miss Smethurst, with Miss Haughton, who taught history, sitting beside her.

The Old Mill, Plumstead Common. This nineteenth-century pub was originally an extension to the windmill where flour was ground until 1853.

The Stringer children in the 1950s. Behind them is their prefab, on Winns Common.

The Lake, Plumstead Common. The authorities had hoped to placate those who were demanding baths at Plumstead in the 1890s by constructing this ornamental lake in Slade Hollow, and an open-air bath at the top of Lakedale Road. The indoor baths were eventually built in Speranza Street in 1907.

The forge known as Jacob's Smithy, on Plumstead Common, c. 1900.

A house in Brookdene Road, Plumstead, decorated for the 1937 coronation. Pictured outside no. 32 are Henry Banks and family.

Olven Road, Plumstead, c. 1928. An ex-serviceman, one of many trying to make a living during the Great Depression, photographed Nora Slaney (left), now Nora Nutkins, outside her home with her friend, Irene Plumtree.

Annual seaside outing of the Links Branch (Plumstead) Women's Co-operative Guild, 1924. Those in the charabanc include Mrs Knight, Mrs Croucher, Mrs Beachy, Mrs Davis, Mrs Cable, Mrs Gower and Mrs Kitchenham. The child on the left is Nora Slaney.

Two views of Plumstead High Street in bygone days. The photograph above was taken in 1882, when the streets were lit by gas lamps and there is not a vehicle in sight (other than the horse and cart!). The picture below is somewhat later, to judge by the tram-lines, the ornate lamp-posts, and the trees planted along the pavement.

Burrage Road, Plumstead, in the first decades of this century. The substantial houses were built in 1849 and occupied by professional people. Further down on the right is St James' Church, now used as the Greenwich Young People's Theatre.

Cottages at the top of Kings Highway, on Winns Common. The area was named after Thomas Winn, who owned cottages and fields here in the nineteenth century. In the middle of the common there is a prehistoric burial mound.

Two views near the Plume of Feathers, Plumstead High Street. The pub was built in the early eighteenth century and retains some of its original architectural features. The horse-drawn tram in the top picture is passing the pub's tea-garden entrance, *c.* 1910, where tea, coffee and refreshments could be bought in the 'Swiss Cottage'.

Sutcliffe Road, Plumstead, *c.* 1900. In this delightful photograph many of the children seem to be posing in their Sunday best clothes. The girl wearing a hat in the centre is pushing a small child in a wicker push-chair, while the other girl holds a metal hoop.

Lakedale Road, 1960s. The public house on the left is The Brewery Tap, situated next to Beasley's Brewery which closed in 1965. The once-famous slogan 'Go to work on an egg' can be seen on the hoarding beneath the RACS clock-tower.

An infants' class in Conway School, 1926. This imposing building with two towers was built by the London School Board in 1897.

Plumcroft School, Plum Lane, 1954. Clearly a Wednesday afternoon when boys and girls were segregated to do woodwork or needlework. A picture of the recently crowned Queen Elizabeth is pinned to the back wall. In the front row on the left is Jacky Bunce who, as Mrs Franklin, now teaches at the same school. Other remembered faces include Joan Ayres, Barbara Johnston, Linda Small, Isabelle Hutchinson, Susan and Ann Sloper, Gisela Galway, Kristina Francis and Jean Fardon.

A class of 8–14-year-old girls from Plum Lane School on a school trip, 1926. Phyllis Brett, who died in 1995, is third from the right in the front row.

Class Eight, Woolwich Central School, Bloomfield Road, 1930–31. The teacher on the left is the father of Mary Quant, the dress designer. The building is now used by the boys of Woolwich Polytechnic School.

A Sunday School outing from The People's Hall, in the Slade, an Evangelical Free Church, 1920s. Mr Bradshaw started his charabanc business from his shop in Lakedale Road, putting wooden seats in his fruit and vegetable van.

A day trip from the Kirkham Street Working Men's Club, probably just after the First World War. These outings were very important, as most children did not have a holiday.

Two Plumstead streets celebrate the coronation of King George VI in 1937. In the top picture, Charles and Alice Potter stand outside their corner shop in Delvan Street with Alice's son, Charles. The shop sold everything from sweets to paraffin oil. The picture below is of Dicey Street. Both streets have now disappeared, replaced by the Woolwich Common Estate.

Eglinton Road School at the time of the 1937 coronation. Many of the surrounding streets have gone, but the school still remains. Built by the London School Board in 1885, it stands on the site of a roller-skating rink and public hall where Mr Gladstone delivered his last speech to Greenwich constituents in 1878.

Coupland Terrace, 1937. A street party to celebrate George VI's coronation.

Alderton's bakery was well known in the Plumstead area. The shop stood for years in Herbert Road, on the corner of the alleyway that led down to Westdale Road. It was said to be the first to market ready-made puff pastry. The baker's cart, below, was distinguished by its smart black and yellow check livery. This picture was taken on Winns Common.

The People's Hall at the Slade, early this century. This Evangelical Free Church was once known as the Slade Mission. It was built by voluntary labour in the 1880s, mostly using bricks from the nearby brickfields in King's Highway. The hall received church status in 1921, thanks to the Revd Mathers. He died during missionary work to the Congo in 1923.

The original nineteenth-century All Saints' Church, at the top of Ripon Road. Both the church and its school were bombed beyond repair in the Second World War. A church hall in Herbert Road was used for Sunday worship until 1957, when a new simple red-brick church was built at the bottom of Ripon Road.

Shooters Hill water tower, built 1910. A familiar landmark for miles around, it cost £3,256 to build, enabling the Metropolitan Water Board to provide a constant supply of water to the increasing number of residents on the hill. In this picture, a steam roller can be seen on the snowy brow of the hill.

Second World War prefabs, next to the water tower. The gardens were well kept, with picket gates and trellises covered with roses.

Children at the back of Christ Church School, Shooters Hill, *c.* 1954. The original 'village' school was built in 1857 but had had some post-war extensions. Fourth from the left is Rick Bruce, with his mother on the right.

Donaldson Road, 1930s. This was part of the hilly Wimpey Estate, built in the 1930s for the increasing population on the slopes of Shooters Hill. It is remarkable to contemporary eyes for the lack of parked cars. Each house was built with a garage space at the rear.

A Wimpey house, inside and out, from a 1933 estate agent's catalogue. Hundreds of houses like this were built in Donaldson Road, Moordown and Ankerdine Crescent; the top price was £695. They have a great deal to recommend them, despite the many steps. These houses have some of the best views in London, overlooking the River Thames.

Shrewsbury House, 1905. This eighteenth-century mansion was once the home of the Earl of Shrewsbury. It was the site of Mr Winser's experiment in gas lighting in 1810. Demolished in 1923, the builder Frederic Halse was responsible for the house we see today, which is used as a community centre.

Shrewsbury Lane, 1907. An amazingly rural scene, hardly comparable with today's busy thoroughfare. Fences hid the large houses from view. The lane led to the Shrewsbury House Estate.

The children's pond on Eaglesfield, *c.* 1912. For years the pond was used as a paddling pool and for sailing motor boats. It has recently been developed into a children's playground.

Eaglesfield's lily-pond, now alas neglected and full of weeds. The highest point of Shooters Hill is at Eaglesfield, which is over 400 ft above sea level and has fine views.

Shrewsbury Park VE Day party, 1945. The party was organized by the residents of Laing's Estate, which backs onto the park. The only uniform to be seen (back row, left) is worn by RAF Officer Bines. In the front row are, among others, Christopher and Elizabeth Grant, Helen Bishop, Jill Batley and Barry Batley.

The Red Lion public house, built in 1902. A horse waits outside the smithy, on the left. The pub is at the centre of Red Lion Place which contains a number of interesting nineteenth-century houses.

The Shooters Hill crossroads, looking down Well Hall Road, *c*. 1900. A dangerous place to stand today! A red-brick police station was built on the far corner in 1915, next to the old police station of 1852. Centuries ago this was the site of the public gallows.

The Royal Herbert (Military) Hospital in Shooters Hill Road. It was built by Sir Douglas Galton in 1865 as the general hospital of the artillery garrison at Woolwich. Inspired by Prince Albert, it is said to have been built to plans intended for a hospital in India, hence the high ceilings and tall arches. The design possibly owes something to Florence Nightingale, too, with its wards in separate pavilions leading off long corridors. The hospital closed in 1978 and has now been converted into luxury apartments, but is little changed externally.

ELTHAM

Lee Road, at Eltham Green, early 1900s. Hay carts, possibly from Middle Park Farm, trundle along the country lanes.

Eltham High Street, 1880. A Royal Mail cart stands by Loney's, the butcher. Sherard House, on the right, was built in 1634. The spire of St John's can be seen behind the trees.

Walter Porteous standing at the door of his corn-merchant's shop, no. 3 Eltham High Street, late 1920s.

Jubilee Cottages, Outtrim's Yard, Eltham, built 1833. The caged bird enjoys the sun while the lamp-mender goes about his business.

Ceremony of New Bells at St John's, Eltham parish church. The 'old six' bells were recast in 1924 and two higher bells were added to a steel frame that replaced the wooden one. The parish beadle stands in the centre.

Ram Alley, near Roper Street in
Eltham. This was one of a maze of
alleyways behind the High Street,
typical of a Kentish village. All these
old streets on the north side of the
High Street have disappeared,
replaced in 1936 by Hinds, the
department store, now Allders.

Bailey's dairy, Middle Park Farm, 1917. Fred Ottley (left) and Fred Marshall are pictured here. The farm was well known in the 1860s for breeding thoroughbred racehorses.

Chapel Farm, Eltham, *c.* 1900. A truly rural scene that is hard to imagine today, transformed as it is into the houses and playing fields of Mottingham, with the roar of traffic from the Sidcup bypass constantly in the background.

Eltham station, in the nineteenth century with its well-tended platforms and flower-beds surrounded by white-washed stones. The lady below waits outside the station in the equivalent of today's chauffeur-driven car.

'Nell Gwynn's Cottage', Eltham Well Hall, next to the First World War hutments, 1920s.

Unlucky thirteen! A car hits hutment 13 in 1935. These 'temporary' hutments were built in Well Hall for the Woolwich Arsenal munitions workers in the First World War. Like the prefabs of the Second World War, they continued to serve as homes for some years after the war was over.

Craigton Road, Well Hall, Eltham, soon after the houses were built in 1914. The builder was Cameron Corbett, who used Scottish names for the streets in which his houses were built.

Dumbreck Road, Eltham, another road of substantial Corbett houses. An early motor car can be seen at the bottom of the road.

The crossroads of Eltham Hill, Eltham High Street and Court Yard, *c.* 1916. Some of the buildings are still there: Mellins the Chemist is now a wine bar, and the Greyhound public house, once a coaching inn, remains to this day. It originally housed the livery stables of Thomas Tilling, well known for his horse-drawn bus service. The weather-boarded building on the corner was Whistler & Worge, auctioneers. The building now on this site is a public house, The Bankers Draft.

The post office, Passey Place, *c.* 1916. Its full title was Eltham Post & Telegraph Office. The building has recently been converted into a public house, appropriately called The Old Post Office. Passey Place is now a very busy side street, a no-through-road, but always bustling with people and traffic.

ACKNOWLEDGEMENTS

We are indebted to many who helped us with this book, either by lending us photos or by giving us information and advice. We would like especially to thank:

Eric Allchurch, the Chandler family, L. and M. Gayton, Liz Lloyd, Barbara Ludlow, Daisy Jerome, Ursula Stuart Mason, Mr Richard, Sue Roberts, Mr Shaw, Joyce Stringer, Alan Turner and the Royal Arsenal Historical Association, Sidney Watson, Whiffen photographers, and Michael Wright.

Many thanks also to Dr Terry Powley, Principal of the Greenwich Community College, and to Julian Watson and his staff at Woodlands, the Local History Library.

Above all, our sincere and grateful thanks to Frances Ward, also at Woodlands, who gave so generously of her time and expertise throughout the project.